THEN & NOW

LIBERTYVILLE

OPPOSITE: The intersection of Church Street and Milwaukee Avenue has been a bustling downtown corner since Libertyville began. The Public Service Building, constructed in 1928, housed the Libertyville Federal Savings and Loan in the 1950s. Fifty years later, the building, now offering financial services as Harris Bank, was restored and listed on the National Register of Historic Places. On the right, Jochim's Corner Cafe, later Proctor's Chatterbox Café, was a popular teen hangout in the 1950s. Presently Lovin Oven Cakery offers Libertyville residents good eats at the same location. (Courtesy of the Libertyville-Mundelein Historical Society.)

THEN & NOW

LIBERTYVILLE

Laura Hickey,
Arlene Lane, and
Sonia Schoenfield

Laura dedicates this book to her parents for their unfailing support and to her Uncle Don for suggesting, "Laura, you should write a book." And so she did.

For Arlene's loving family—Adam, Justin, Tina, Briar, and Joseph; for Greg, who would have been proud; and for Jim, who lights up her life.

Sonia dedicates this book to Peter, Carl, and Claire, with love and thankfulness for our then and now, and with great anticipation for the future. Hebrews 13:8.

ISBN 978-0-7385-8389-1

Library of Congress Control Number: 2010928306

Published by Arcadia Publishing
Charleston, South Carolina

Printed in the United States of America

For all general information, please contact Arcadia Publishing:
Telephone 843-853-2070
Fax 843-853-0044
E-mail sales@arcadiapublishing.com
For customer service and orders:
Toll-Free 1-888-313-2665

Visit us on the Internet at www.arcadiapublishing.com

On the Front Cover: Petranek's Pharmacy was a successor to the historic Lovell's Pharmacy, owned by Kenneth Lovell, which opened for business at that site in 1876. Louis J. Petranek took over in the late 1940s, and the business became Petranek's in 1950. A fire in 1954 did $125,000 worth of damage, destroying the Lovell Building; it reopened in 1956. A series of owners took over, continuing to operate under the name Petranek's as the only independent pharmacy in the area. (Above, courtesy of Laura Hickey; below, courtesy of the Libertyville-Mundelein Historical Society.)

On the Back Cover: In a quintessential scene of 1950s small-town daily life, a local paperboy hand delivers the newspaper to the home of Miss Anna Appley. "Annie," as she was known to her friends, was a lifetime resident of Libertyville whose family history is intertwined with that of her beloved hometown. (Courtesy of the Libertyville-Mundelein Historical Society.)

Contents

Acknowledgments

We wish to thank the Libertyville-Mundelein Historical Society for their generosity in sharing photographs and information. We are especially appreciative of Audrey Krueger, archivist for the society, and Pres. Faith Sage for their patience with our many requests. Several of the society's members contributed very useful information, and for that we are eternally grateful.

We would also like to thank Anne and David Howard, Jack Forney, and Charles Bresley. Thank you for allowing us to accompany you on a trip down memory lane. It was truly a pleasure to share the experience with you; your information was invaluable. We are particularly thankful for Jack Forney's generosity in sharing his personal collection of historical artifacts from his time of employment with the Frank G. Hough Company. We are grateful for the many responses from alumni of Libertyville High School. The class of 1959 was especially helpful in providing answers to our inquiries. Specifically we thank Dr. Robert Buttemiller, Franco Alhaique, Bettye Lukenbill, and Marlene Edman Fischer.

Other informational sources for this publication include the *Independent Register*, Libertyville directories, Libertyville High School yearbooks, local businesses, townspeople, and the local history files at Cook Memorial Public Library.

The majority of historical photographs in this book are courtesy of the Carl C. Cizek Collection from the archives of the Libertyville-Mundelein Historical Society. We would like to thank the late Carl Cizek for thinking of future generations when he went on his 1950s adventure to capture Libertyville on film. Other vintage images are courtesy of Jack Forney's personal collection. Laura Hickey took all of the contemporary photographs. We give a special thanks to Laura's photography assistant, driver, and creative contributor, Darlene Hickey.

Lastly, we are grateful to Marlon Brando for bringing the three of us together on our quest to preserve Libertyville's past for future generations.

Introduction

Libertyville was born in the 1840s near the Des Plaines River along an old American Indian trail from Chicago to Milwaukee. In the 1950s, Libertyville reflected an optimism that dominated the country, welcoming development and progress with open arms, transitioning from a small community to a suburb with its eyes on the future. Business was booming. New schools and churches were being built. The future was bright. Today Libertyville has grown to a suburban village of 22,000 in the heart of the northern Chicago metropolitan region.

In its early history, Libertyville was built by hardworking pioneers who farmed or owned businesses. In the 1950s, farming was still an important part of local life and the local economy. Large estates such as John Cuneo's Hawthorn Mellody Farm raised prize cattle and dairy cows. Red Top, the John Allen farm, was known for its thoroughbred horses. Just northwest of town was the Quaker Oats experimental farm, which produced Ful-O-Pep chicken feed and hosted The Man on the Farm radio program on Chicago station WLS. Today most farms have been given over to development, although a few still dot the landscape in and beyond the village limits.

Libertyville grew up along Milwaukee Avenue, a major stagecoach route in its early days. In the late 1800s, the community banded together to bring rail service to the village, thus securing a connection with Chicago, Milwaukee, and the world beyond. In the 1950s, those same rail lines brought both steam and electric rail service, providing transportation for commuters to Chicago. The tollway was being built just east of town. Today the electric rail line no longer exists, although the track line is now a path for walkers, joggers, and bicyclists. Commuters still ride the train to their Chicago jobs, and the tollway is part of a major thoroughfare between Indiana and Wisconsin.

In 1895, a fire swept through downtown Libertyville and many of the downtown business buildings were destroyed. Quite a few of the buildings that were constructed after the fire are still part of the downtown scenery today, including the Proctor, Gridley, and Heath Buildings, among others. In the 1950s, those buildings were home to many family-owned businesses, as well as chains such as Woolworth's and A&P. Today few of these businesses remain, and the commercial district has moved beyond downtown.

However, the buildings have been preserved. Libertyville has worked hard to attract and keep businesses in the downtown area, and today those sturdy brick buildings are alive with eager shoppers.

Although family-owned businesses have always played a part in Libertyville's economy, the village has been host to light industry as well. Factories like Foulds have been around for 100 years. Others like Anchor Coupling, Brown Paper Goods, Burgess Manning, Frank G. Hough, Morton Manufacturing, and Onsrud Cutter came on the scene later but have endured. Hough and Foulds were particularly known for the positive impact they had on their community and for the personal relationships they established with their employees.

Other examples of Libertyville's optimistic spirit have carried over from the 1950s to now. During that period, the Cook Memorial Public Library, housed in the home of Ansel B. Cook, held a place of honor in Cook Park. In the ensuing years, the library grew into a district and moved into a new building just behind the Cook House. This building is now being expanded and renovated. Ansel Cook's home has become a first-class Victorian museum filled with furniture, clothing, and other objects from the time period.

Condell Memorial Hospital, built in 1928 with private and public funds, had a humble beginning in a farm field south of town. In the 1950s, it underwent two major expansions, again with enthusiastic community backing. Today the hospital is the only Level I trauma center in the area, and expansion plans continue to meet the need for quality health care.

In the 1950s, the automobile was king. There was a service station on just about every corner and automobiles were a hot commodity, from new and used dealers to repair and parts stores. Today, south of downtown, Milwaukee Avenue is lined with car dealerships, and even in tough economic times they are a source of revenue for the village.

Many politicians have passed through Libertyville over the years, and one even made his home here. In the early 1900s, Illinois governor Charles Samuel Deneen campaigned on the main street. Rural Libertyville was home to Adlai Stevenson when he served as Illinois governor, ran for president, and held the post of U.S. ambassador to the United Nations. Stevenson hosted many political celebrities to his Libertyville farm, notably Eleanor Roosevelt and John F. Kennedy, who spoke on the steps of the Cook House during his 1960 presidential campaign. In 1976, Betty Ford visited Lambs Farm, a residential facility for developmentally disabled adults, during her husband's presidential campaign.

Hollywood has left its mark on Libertyville also. During World War II, in response to Libertyville's tremendous support of the war bond drive, James Cagney danced on the steps of the Cook House. Helen Keller also visited to make an appeal in a war-bond drive. A young Marlon Brando attended the Libertyville-Fremont Township High School in the 1940s, the same high school that was used as a backdrop for the 2001 film *New Port South*.

The heart of any community is its schools, churches, and civic organizations, and Libertyville is no different than most. In the booming 1950s, two schools were built to accommodate the growth in school-aged children, both from the baby boom and the village's population boom. Churches of a variety of denominations have served the residents of Libertyville since its inception. In the 1950s, several churches underwent expansion and new buildings were constructed.

With the increase in leisure time in the 1950s, opportunities to participate in civic and recreational activities flourished. Men, women, and children enjoyed a variety of activities in clubs and auxiliaries and religious and civic organizations, as well as athletic and homegrown clubs. Teens went to the movies or cheered at school sports. Today many of these pastimes have been taken up by a new generation. A commitment to community involvement persists as sports, scouting, civic activities, and the arts are strongly supported. Teens still meet each other at the movies, and homecoming endures as one of Libertyville's biggest events of the year.

Libertyville continues to exert an emotional pull on its residents, past and present. We share a portion of the poem "Where Dreams Begin" by Marlene Edman Fischer, class of 1954: "So I'll close my eyes and travel awhile, / And visit past days, and smile. / 'Cause this I know, where'er thoughts roam, / Libertyville is my home."

We offer this book as a tribute to the men and women who have built our village from the beginning. Former residents who grew up in Libertyville will see Then & Now: *Libertyville* as a personal scrapbook of their lives. Current business owners will be interested in seeing how their buildings have changed or how they have survived. The buildings depicted in this book create a backdrop for the lives of all who have passed through them and by them, a backdrop to generations from Libertyville, then and now.

CHAPTER 1

Bringin' Home the Bacon

In 1950s Libertyville, the community thrived on its many industrial companies, including lumberyards, machine factories, and food plants. Workers were loyal to their employers and, in turn, their employers loyal to them. A fine example was the Frank G. Hough Company (pictured). Hough hired only returning GIs, paying them, according to Jack Forney, "A nickel higher than average."

Frank G. Hough Company was primarily responsible for the development of the first fully integrated wheel loader. For more than a decade, the company produced industry-defining innovations, such as four-wheel drive, torque conversion, and hydrostatic transmission. Along with industrial relations manager Jack Forney, Frank Hough was instrumental in creating Adler Park. The company was sold to International Harvester in 1952, but Hough loaders were still manufactured for 30 years. Hanna Cylinder relocated all manufacturing operations to this location in 2004.

Morton Manufacturing Company is part of the industrial base of Libertyville's economy. Morton is a family-owned business begun in 1903. It located to Libertyville in 1942. By 1951, the company had 130 employees, and its product line included steel kitchen cabinets. Today its inventory includes antislip metal walkways, stair treads, and ladder rungs for the railroad, construction, and farming industries.

The Foulds Company, founded in Cincinnati in 1885 by Frank Foulds, opened its pasta production in Libertyville in 1905. The building (originally a ladder factory) was constructed in part with timber from the 1893 World's Columbian Exposition. In the early decades, the factory housed the town's fire siren, which alerted volunteer firefighters to report for duty. Foulds also hosted picnics and Christmas parties for the town. Today Foulds continues to produce quality pasta products that appear under other names.

Brown Paper Goods Company came to Libertyville in 1940. In 1951, it employed about 85 people and manufactured many kinds of paper bags, including lunch, refuse, sandwich, and paper bags used for food packaging. Today it is located in Waukegan and continues to manufacture specialty bags and sheets for the food-service industry. Classic Windows, Inc. was founded by Tom Davis and began manufacturing high-quality windows and doors for residential and commercial projects in 1992.

Sherman Coy opened Coy Lumber in the 1940s. The property had formerly been home to Franzen Lumber. Coy's company sold lumber, millwork, insulation, roofing, building materials, and coal. He was so well respected that upon hearing the news of his sudden death on February 15, 1946, all Libertyville stores closed their doors for an hour of mourning. After his death, Sherman's son Edward took over the business until 1963. Currently MainStreet Libertyville occupies the offices of Coy Lumber.

The Libertyville Lumber Company was established in 1903 and provided quality wood products for almost 100 years. The company was located on a spur of the Milwaukee Railroad. The train tracks ran into a lumber warehouse paved with old-time Chicago street bricks. In the 1950s, the company offered additional building material products such as doors and drywall. In 2004, the site was demolished and a brick condominium development, Heritage Place, was built by Cambridge Homes.

The Anchor Coupling Company manufactured high- and low-pressure hoses and assemblies. Its product line was used for a wide variety of construction and handling equipment, automobiles, and defense equipment. The "coupling" in the Anchor name represented the fittings used on the ends of hose assemblies. In the 1950s, the company was well established in this building on Fourth Avenue. It was later noted as a supplier for the U.S. space project. Amerace Limited took over Anchor Coupling in 1976.

In 1920, Oscar Onsrud invented the humble router, a tool many take for granted. In fact, Onsrud held many mechanical patents. He opened his cutter manufacturing factory in Libertyville in 1925. By 1951, he employed 33 people and specialized in high-speed steel, solid carbide, and carbide-tipped cutters for the woodworking and aircraft industries. The privately owned company is still in business today, and its cutting tools are distributed throughout the world.

Telephone service came to Libertyville in 1897 when F. B. Lovell and Fletcher Clark formed the Lake County Telephone Company. The back room of Lovell's drugstore was the central office with one operator. By 1929, telephone service was provided at this site from a rented building. This building was constructed to meet increased demand for telephone service after the war; completion allowed for expanded and modernized services, including conversion to dial service by 1950. No more party lines!

CHAPTER 2

Be True to Your School

School spirit is abundant in Libertyville. The majority of the town's youth work their way through the public school system, finishing their education as Wildcats at Libertyville High School. Pictured are students cheering outside of the Brainerd Building's Jackson Gym. Brainerd opened in 1917 as Libertyville Township High School, and the Jackson Gym was added on in 1920.

The Brainerd Building served as a four-year high school from 1917 to 1955. Notably, Marlon Brando attended school here and Helen Keller visited in the 1940s. With the opening of a new high school building in 1954, Brainerd became freshmen-only. In 1998, the facility housed its last class of freshmen and has been vacant since 2003. On July 16, 2008, the building was listed on the National Register of Historic Places. Currently volunteers are trying to restore Brainerd and convert it into a community center.

With the population booming in the 1950s, Libertyville needed a larger high school. On November 7, 1954, Libertyville-Fremont High School's new $1.48 million Butler Building was dedicated. The chief speaker at the event was former Illinois governor and democratic presidential candidate Adlai E. Stevenson. Since that day, the school has grown, as have its athletic facilities. The district lines have been redrawn and a second high school built. However, one thing remains consistent: Libertyville High School's dedication to quality public education.

With Libertyville's population growing in 1926, Rockland Elementary School opened to educate children from the southern part of town. Rockland served kindergarten through eighth grade until 1950, when Highland Middle School opened next door. The building has had many additions, including extra classrooms and a gymnasium. In the 1990s, the school changed its mascot from the timid Rockland Robin to the ferocious Rockland Raptor. It remains a K-5 grammar school for southern Libertyville residents.

Copeland Elementary School was opened in 1957 to accommodate students from the Copeland Manor subdivision in southeastern Libertyville. The area had originally been part of the extensive farm holdings of Charles C. Copeland. The school was designed to serve students from kindergarten through fifth grade. Over the years, as the population grew, the school was enlarged to include more classrooms, a library, a gym, and playing fields and playgrounds. Current enrollment is almost 400 students.

Construction on Highland School began in 1949 and was completed in time for the beginning of the 1950 school year. Built at a cost of $496,000, the school was called "streamlined" and demonstrated the latest in classroom equipment and planning. At the time, the school was located on 13 acres with athletic space, an ice-skating rink, and a putting green. The school remains a forerunner for education of grades six through eight with a newly installed solar panel that teaches green efficiency.

The original Central School was constructed in 1886. In 1939, it was razed and a new Georgian-style facility was built. A copper box time capsule was placed within the cornerstone of the building. It contained newspaper clippings, textbooks, coins, and a letter from Supt. Carl W. Baylor. The school served elementary students until 1984. During the 1990s, it housed an alternative high school. Currently it is vacant with plans to be remodeled into condominiums.

After many years of consideration, construction started in 1925 on St. Joseph Catholic School. The building, designed by Hyland and Corse, was built at a cost of $80,000. The school opened in 1926 with an enrollment of 150 children. In 1957, ground was broken on a new expansion project adding classrooms, a convent, chapel, and one of the largest grammar school gymnasiums in the archdiocese. With many expansions, the school continues to serve as a kindergarten through eighth educational facility.

CHAPTER 3

SUNDAY GO TO MEETIN'

Libertyville's religious roots grow deep. Just a year after the town was settled, the Methodist church was organized. In 1866, Methodists built the Union Church with Congregationalists, Presbyterians, Baptists, and Universalists. Today there are many diverse congregations. This nativity scene, purchased for holiday viewing in 1954, is a religious tradition that has continued to the present day.

This was the site of Union Church, constructed in 1868. It was built as a common meeting place for many religious organizations. St. Lawrence Church purchased the property in 1913. In 1917, a fire destroyed the entire building. Despite scarce lumber supplies due to the impending war, church members were able to construct a new sanctuary by the end of the year. An education wing was added in 1963–1964. Recently an expansion project doubled the usable space of the building.

The Methodist congregation was organized in Libertyville in 1836. In 1913, the United Methodist Church moved to the brick building pictured below. Sometime after 1945, Paul and Marian Pettingill presented the church with a set of Carillonic bells in memory of their esteemed fathers, Dr. John Taylor and Charles Pettingill. From the tower, the bells could be heard a mile away. The original structure was razed in 1967. The current, larger sanctuary was built in its place that same year.

The first wood-framed Catholic church in Libertyville tragically burned in 1904; it was rebuilt at its current location. On July 2, 1905, auxiliary bishop Peter J. Muldoon dedicated the new brick church as St. Joseph. It had the capacity for 300 people at the time, and by the 1960s the parish had grown to 1,000 families. The original brick building was razed to make room for an entirely new, modern church. In the 2000s, the building was renovated to further accommodate its worshipers.

This building was constructed as a small frame church in 1905. It was home to St. John Lutheran Church until 1950. The Christian Science Society was established in Libertyville in 1923. In 1944, as the membership grew, the group became the First Church of Christian Scientist. In April 1950, the Christian Scientists purchased and remodeled the former St. John Church. A fire extensively damaged the structure in 1980. It was reconstructed and enlarged to its current state.

St. John Lutheran Church was dedicated on April 20, 1952. Walter Kroeber of Arlington Heights was the architect of this English Gothic–style church. The exterior is of Lannon stone with Bedford limestone trim, and the interior is natural oak wood. St. John Lutheran, organized in 1897, first worshipped in the Union Church and then a small frame building on Park Place that was sold to the First Church of Christ Scientist in 1950.

The Libertyville Evangelical Free Church was formed in January 1951. Congregants met in homes, then in the American Legion Hall. In 1955, they purchased 10 acres of land at the southeast corner of Austin and Garfield Avenues. A parsonage was constructed in 1956, and in January 1957 they broke ground for a new church, where they held their first worship service in July 1958. The congregation continued to grow, and in 1989 they added a new, 500-seat sanctuary.

Libertyville's Presbyterian Church was organized in 1886. The first building was constructed on East Church Street on land formerly owned by Horace Butler. In 1925, the congregation bought land at the corner of Douglas Street and Maple Avenue. The building erected thereon was dedicated in 1928. Over the years, the building was expanded and in 1955 adjoining property was purchased. This education building was erected and dedicated in 1961. The church remains an active part of the Libertyville community today.

CHAPTER 4

Takin' Care of Business

Main Street is not a cliché in Libertyville—it is a reality. From its beginnings, the town was built around Milwaukee Avenue. Residents could walk up and down the street and pass drugstores, clothing shops, grocery stores, restaurants, a park, and the library. The store names may have changed, but the heart of the town endures on Milwaukee Avenue.

The Liberty Theatre has been here since August 27, 1937, when owner Fred Dobe opened the doors of his new, 700-seat, air-conditioned building. Designed in the art moderne style by E. P. Rupert, the architecture featured a terra-cotta exterior with dark blue trim. In the 1950s, the marquee advertised films starring the theater's most famous employee, Marlon Brando, who worked there as an usher between 1939 and 1941. "Modernized" later, the theater now reflects a vintage 1970s look.

Kitchener Lund and his wife, Ivy, owned Lund's Restaurant. They died tragically in a car accident in 1966. Henry Yee's Cantonese restaurant was established in 1961 and became a well-known fixture downtown. Former residents remember the candy store next door where they used to stop before heading to the Liberty Theatre. Henry Yee's was sold in 2007, and although the new owners kept the name, they remodeled and changed the cuisine to Szechuan and Hunan.

Barbers have been cutting men's hair at this location since 1916. Today the Vojtech and Rivers families, who have owned the business since 1950, continue to provide a good haircut and retain a loyal customer base. Next door, the Village Jeweler, in business since 1985, was the former site of Western Tire and Auto Shop. The store sold tires and accepted trade-ins. It was one of the many businesses that catered to automobile owners and enthusiasts.

The Sportsman came into being when Clavey's Hardware Store decided to put all of its sporting goods on sale in one spot in 1950. In 1951, The Sportsman was at 110 Lake Street. It moved to 608 North Milwaukee Avenue in 1952 and remained in business until the 1980s. Everyone, it seemed, bought their sports equipment at The Sportsman. It sold equipment for archery, golf, tennis, hockey, baseball, football, and basketball, as well as guns and ammunition and fishing tackle.

In the 1950s, downtown Libertyville boasted at least three grocery stores, including Phil Bogue's IGA. The IGA was open seven days a week and took phone orders for door-to-door delivery. It closed in the 1960s. Trattoria Pomigliano opened at this site in 1994. It is owned by the Saladino and Panico families and features Ann Panico's home recipes of southern Italian cuisine from the Naples region. The restaurant is named after the Italian town where Ann's husband was born.

This building, constructed in 1903, originally housed a theater on the upper floors and First National Bank at street level. A merger caused the eventual name change to First State Bank. Also on the lower level in the 1950s, Taylor Furniture Mart boasted three floors of showrooms and offered discounted furniture at 20 to 40 percent off on national brands. Since 1974, Dancenter North has occupied the upper floors of the building. Avenue 21 Dancewear and Starbucks Coffee can be found downstairs.

F. W. Woolworth's, a national branch five-and-dime store, opened in Libertyville's Proctor Building in the 1930s. After renovations, on June 28, 1940, the store reopened with modern lighting and ventilation throughout its 5,000 square feet of floor space. At the time, it was the largest retail shop in town. The store sold miscellaneous goods at inexpensive prices. It remained open until the late 1970s. Currently a clothing boutique, Street Chic, and home accent shop, Motif, occupy the space.

The 1903 Proctor Building, declared "Libertyville's First Metropolitan Building" by the *Independent Register*, housed the New Castle Hotel for over 90 years. Tenants in the 1950s included optometrist Ray Woodworth and Factor's women's apparel store, which extended into the alley. Lulu Duddles had closed off the alley in 1932 for additional retail space. In the late 1990s, building renovation restored the alleyway and converted hotel rooms into apartments. Someone's in the Kitchen is a gourmet cook shop offering cooking classes.

Originally H. B. Eger's Hardware, by the 1950s this was Ace Hardware and owned by Ernie Griffis and later Paul Hesse. In the 1960s, they consolidated with Schanck Hardware next door, keeping the Ace name. Chandler's was the local stationery shop where everyone bought their school supplies.

Townee Square, owned by George and Christine Karahalios, has served breakfast and lunch to a loyal local following since it moved into the vacant building in 1986. Studio West has been in business since 1969.

In 1870, George Schank established his hardware and implement company at this location, an enterprise that soon made him a prosperous business leader. When the great Libertyville fire of 1895 destroyed Schank's, George rebuilt the brick building pictured here that still bears his name. The hardware business changed hands but continued through the next century. In 1962, Paul Hesse consolidated Schank's with Ace Hardware, a local business in operation today on Peterson Road. Soccer Plus now occupies the landmark corner.

A&P Company Food Store, the first nationally known chain store, opened a shop in Libertyville's Proctor Building in the 1920s. Later the grocery store moved to newer and larger quarters at this location. Sometime in the late 1950s, A&P closed due to supermarket competition. Arden's Fine Furniture and Design moved here in 1960 and has sold fine furniture in this building for 50 years. Carla Davidovic and Mike Maine currently own Arden's.

The Park View remained a tavern from 1935 to 1973. From 1973 to 1983, the name changed to Flagg's Tavern after its new owner, Tom Flagg. Coincidently, Tom's grandfather Lew operated a barbershop in the same building in the 1920s and early 1930s. Mickey Finn's moved in during the mid-1980s and began a microbrewery in 1994. Founders Bill Sugars and Pat Elmquest sold to Brian Grano, the current owner of the popular watering hole.

Jay's Shoes sold Buster Brown and Stride Rite shoes for children, plus women's and men's footwear. Customers buying shoes at Jay's also meant seeing their feet through the x-ray machine. Julian Redman advertised his eponymous boys' and menswear store as "Home of Famous Brands." He opened his menswear business here in the mid-1950s, moved to South Milwaukee a decade later, and stayed in business into the 1990s. Today this location hosts Murphy's, a popular health food store, and Magic Touch Cleaners.

The beautiful Public Service Building was constructed by utilities magnate Samuel Insull and designed by noted Prairie School architect Hermann V. Von Holst. Shortly after the building's dedication in 1928, the stock market crashed and Insull went bankrupt. The building fell into disrepair until the 1950s, when the Libertyville Savings and Loan Association purchased the structure and modernized it with a flat facade. After an exterior restoration, the building was added to the National Register of Historic Places in 1983.

Scottie's was located in front of the Cardinal Bus Lines stop near Broadway and Milwaukee Avenue, which was a spot that provided some added business for the restaurant. In the 1950s, Scottie's advertised home-cooked specials, including "country style chicken" and "club steaks." Huffman's, a milk and grocery store, was established by Edwin Huffman and later managed by his son-in-law Ed Young. The store also provided home delivery for Hawthorn Mellody Farm products. A wine shop and nail salon take their place today.

Vondracek's specialized in the sale of radios and televisions and offered repairs during an era when tubes could be easily and economically replaced. Paul Senthen owned a popular barbershop, and Willis Overholser and associates operated a law office in the same building. Overholser used his office to organize the first local Lions Club chapter in 1933. Lion Overholser Park is dedicated in his name. How Impressive, Awards and Engraving, and Upscale Resale reside in the building now.

Ruttkay Jewelers sold diamonds, fine jewelry, watches, and gifts for brides-to-be. Boehm-Schreck provided a complete range of insurance coverage for local customers. Otto Boehm started his independent insurance business in 1918, and his son George joined him in 1956. In the 1950s, Ray Shreck, a State Farm agent, joined Otto for a short time in an experimental partnership. Boehm and Ray Insurance still exists today and George Boehm is semiretired. A custom-design gown shop and Canyon Kitchens reside here now.

J. C. Reuse was a real estate sales, insurance, and property management company established in 1935 by Joseph Reuse and his assistant, Ila Haven. A former close advisor of Samuel Insull, Reuse was in charge of Insull's interests in Lake County and served as president of the bank in the Insull-established Public Service Building. Joseph Reuse managed his own business from 1933 until his death in 1946, when Ila Haven assumed ownership. A flower shop graces the corner now.

In 1920, Emil Mesenbrink moved to Libertyville, purchased a greenhouse on First Street, and started the Libertyville Floral Company. Later he moved his retail business to more prominent locations on Milwaukee Avenue, finally settling at this location. Emil retired in 1957 and sold his business to Russell Proctor. The building was later demolished and the flower shop moved, but the business still bears the Proctor name today. Peter Tosto constructed the Heritage Courts building standing here now in 1980.

Howard Krueger established Krueger Motors in 1946. The authorized De Soto dealership sold new and used cars until De Soto production slowed in the 1950s. Howard then formed a partnership with another Chrysler dealer, Fred Miller, establishing Miller-Krueger Dodge. The dealership was located for many years at 119 South Milwaukee Avenue in a former recreation center. A local newspaper, the *Independent Register*, later occupied the building pictured here. The current tenants are Edward Jones and Condell Hospital.

Open until midnight, the Chatterbox was a popular restaurant, especially with the younger crowd. Russ Proctor offered a menu of ice cream, hamburgers, sandwiches, waffles, and plate lunches served at a counter and tables; a candy counter sold Mrs. Steven's Chocolates. Kids who skipped school for a snack could run out the back door if they were noticed. Lovin Oven Cakery now resides at this corner. Opened in 2009, the bakery is a third-generation business run by the Slove family.

In 1924, brothers Roy and Harry Titus purchased this building at the corner of Cook Street and Milwaukee Avenue, formerly occupied by the Lake County National Bank. The business, known as an "electric shop," thrived for more than 50 years, becoming Titus Brothers Electrical Contractors. An Italian bakery took over the historic corner when the business closed. The Picnic Basket, owned by the Amin family, arrived in 1981. It remains today as a popular delicatessen-restaurant and Gourmet Food Works catering service.

First Lake County Bank, established in 1892, was the third bank in Lake County. It was organized by Libertyville business leaders who needed quicker access to cash due to prosperous local grain shipments. The building pictured here was completed in 1922. In the 1970s, its facade was hidden beneath a brick wall. Fortunately the brick was eventually removed and the building's stately Grecian styling was restored. Libertyville Bank and Trust is the current occupant.

Petranek's was a successor to Lovell's Pharmacy, founded here by Frank Lovell in 1872. For years, the historic drugstore remained in business, retaining the Lovell name. Shortly after Lou Petranek took over in the late 1940s, he renamed the pharmacy after himself. A fire in 1954 caused $125,000 worth of damage to the original building. While Lou rebuilt, the store temporarily operated here until 1956. Keswick's was a Hallmark Shop forerunner. Firkin and Tavern, fine restaurants, reside here now.

Ray Taylor, a former pharmacist, opened Taylor Paint Store in the 1940s. In 1947, his son-in-law Maynard Seiler came to work for him. A few years later, the store expanded to include hobby items, and the name changed to Taylor and Seiler Paint and Hobbies. Its inventory included the obvious—paints and hobby materials, as well as wallpaper, tools, and toys. In 1973, Taylor retired from the business. Forty years after opening, the store closed. Forest Bootery resides here now.

Earl Langworthy bought W. W. Carroll's dry goods store in 1911 and started a legacy that spanned three generations of his family. Langworthy's became a landmark on Milwaukee Avenue in Libertyville during an 89-year reign. Earl's son Tom took over after World War II, focusing more on quality men's and women's clothing. When Tom's son Terry assumed leadership in the 1970s, Langworthy's became the largest Pendleton brand dealer in northern Illinois. Closed in 2000, Langworthy's is replaced by Adrienne Clarisse.

Flegelman's Department Store, named after owners Jim and Ruth Flegelman, sold clothing and furniture. During the holidays, children visited with Santa while the family shopped. Flegelman's permitted Ray-Burnett to use the space on their upper floor to store their extra caskets, a common arrangement between furniture stores and funeral homes. When Flegelman's closed, Julian Redman, a men's clothing store, opened in its place, and later Langworthy's expanded into the space. Charles and Minerva and Touché Salon are the current tenants.

What began as a grocery store in the early 1900s housed Smith's Shoes for 50 years. Managed by Ray Smith in the 1950s, the store offered brands for all ages, from Jumping Jacks to Red Cross shoes. The store had a shoe-fitting fluoroscope that used an x-ray tube to view a fluorescent image of the bones of the feet. After the store closed, an art gallery briefly opened. Rocky Mountain Chocolate Factory resides in the space.

Italy native Anthony Abbadessa opened Tony's Shoe Shop in 1912. The store's main service was shoe repair. As the only cobbler in town, he never found it necessary to be listed in the phone book. Abbadessa retired in 1962 and passed away a year later. Reinbach Delicatessen was located next door. An advertisement claimed that it gave special attention to wedding and party orders. The business relocated to Waukegan in 1956. Recently the space underwent a complete remodel and is available for lease.

The Wisconsin Packing Company was a food processing wholesaler and retailer. Butchers slaughtered and prepared meats, fish, and poultry on site and rented lockers for frozen food storage. It sold and repaired Philco and Frigidaire freezers and refrigerators, too. Later known as Mundelein Locker Service, the shop closed in 1955 due to bankruptcy. Amazing Cosmetics, a successful makeup line launched in 2000, has won the support of many Hollywood celebrities. A popular sub sandwich shop, Chip's, also shares the current space.

Started in 1914 by John N. Bernard, the longtime Libertyville dealership that became Bernard Chevrolet was originally located at 611 North Milwaukee Avenue. After World War II, Bernard's sons joined the company and business boomed, necessitating a move. In the 1950s, Bernard Motor Sales, seen here, was located at 135 North Milwaukee Avenue, where new and used cars (under the name OK Auto Mart) were purchased and serviced. Manchester Square, a major retail and condominium development, stands here today.

In 1956, Central Auto Service was one of 24 service stations in town. The business opened a decade earlier, occupying the former lot of Merle's Auto Repair. Central remained open for some 20 years. Banzai Motorsports later took over the lot and building next door. A 2003 roof collapse led to the eventual demolition of the building. In 2009, a three-story condominium and retail development was constructed on the prominent corner.

The Dall Building was erected in the mid-1920s (pictured here) along Lake Street and Milwaukee Avenue. The Lueck Sewing Machine Company sold and repaired sewing machines, including the Pfaff brand. Bronx Cleaners was a dry cleaners and self-service launderette. Carol's Cut and Curl was a beauty salon offering mother-daughter service. Two businesses currently occupy the site: Midnight Sun Swedish Antiques, which opened in 2002 and is owned by Annika Christensen, and North Shore Pro-Active Health, a chiropractic wellness clinic.

Adolph Trinko founded his eponymous glass company in 1946. The company sold flat glass for home, commercial, and industrial uses, including custom mirrors and furniture tops. Trinko retired in 1962, and the business closed sometime after 1967. Jenny Sweeney Designs creates custom invitations as well as greeting cards and stationery for sale at over 2,000 retail outlets throughout the country. Its Libertyville location houses offices and a boutique, as well as some manufacturing.

Henry and Ethel Baer opened Libertyville Home Laundry, Inc. in 1939. Fourteen years later, in 1953, they changed the business name to Baer's Laundry and Dry Cleaning. The couple provided many services, including waterproofing, dyeing, "cleaner" dry cleaning with Du Pont's Perchlorethylene system, and pick-up or delivery service. As seen in the photograph, the company's symbol was an upright bear. The business closed in the early 1970s. Recently Angie's Antiques was located here.

Dr. George Buttemiller purchased the 1894 home at 117 Church Street in 1940. The first floor served as his practice and his family resided upstairs. He planned to build his clinic next door, as the business papers were marked 121 West Church Street to save later costs. Instead, the house was converted into a clinic. Dr. Lawrence Day later became his partner. Dr. Buttemiller retired in 1975. The building now serves as the law office of Mayor Terry Weppler.

In 1896, Frank Just acquired the *Lake County Independent*, founded in 1892. It became the *Libertyville Independent Register* in 1930. Just published the paper until his death in 1953. During the 1950s, this building housed the *Independent Register* along with Hampton Greeting Cards, a stationery and card store owned by Just's son-in-law Richard Anderson. The *Independent Register* was published every Thursday, and subscribers eagerly anticipated its delivery of local news. It ceased publication in 1987. Condell Hospice now resides in the building.

This building held the offices of Liberty Insurance and Real Estate and optometrist Dr. Robert E. Sayers. Established in 1923, Liberty Insurance provided mortgages, insurance, management, and appraisals. By 1956, the company was no longer in the building. Dr. Sayers was an optometrist for 26 years preceding his unexpected death in 1961. He was also an antique automobile enthusiast and member of the Village Band. Around 1970, the current tenant, Dan the Key Man locksmiths, moved into the building.

Charlotte's opened in 1951 and moved to the location pictured here in the mid-1950s. With five operators on duty and the benefit of air-conditioning, it was the place for women and children to go for all of their hair-styling needs. Charlotte's advertised color correction for "removal of dyes, tints, compound hennas, metallic dyes, or the effects of amateur color tampering." Its slogan read, "Let your hair tell the world about you." The Village Press offices currently occupy the building.

This location originally housed Wilcox Press, a commercial printer and office-supply business. In 1945, John and Elizabeth Pyle and Bud Gore purchased the business. In 1948, they changed the name to The Village Press. Over the years, their business has gone from strictly commercial printing in the mid-1950s to doing finishing work for other printers in the 1980s. The Village Press remains a family-owned business today.

In the 1950s, Libertyville was full of auto shops where hot-rodders could grease their wheels; Motor Parts and Machine Company was one of them. It opened in 1947 on Lake Street and moved to the location pictured in 1952. The company sold motor parts and machinery to manufacturers and wholesalers. It also offered a complete machine shop service. The business closed in the 1960s. Currently R. E. Decker PC Land Surveyors finds its home in the space.

The Record Shop opened in 1956 just east of the Ace Hardware building. A teen hangout, the shop sold jazz, popular, classical, ethnic, western, folk, and Latin American LP and single phonograph records. Another store under the same management was located in Waukegan. The Libertyville shop remained in business until 1962. A. Perry Designs and Builds, owned by Anthony Perry, is a custom residential design-build firm that opened in May 2008.

The Village Pantry restaurant opened in 1953. Its menu included homemade pies, breakfast, hamburgers, plate lunches, club steaks, homemade soups, and spaghetti every Wednesday. One of its ads read, "We seat 1500 people—15 at a time!" In 1958, the restaurant closed its doors at that address and the Village Restaurant opened across the street with the same Wednesday spaghetti special. Currently the Christian Science Reading room, a bookstore and space for spiritual exploration, occupies the building.

CHAPTER 5

THIS 'N THAT

When villagers were not occupied with work, there were plenty of other activities to keep them busy. Bowling and golf leagues were top choices in sports. A wide variety of clubs met every interest, and parks and lakes offered recreation for all ages. Everyone knew their neighbors, had fun together, took care of each other, and at times grieved together too.

Television shows in the 1950s like *Championship Bowling* caused a surge in the sport's popularity. Al and Tony Cavalier operated the Libertyville Recreation Center, a 10-lane bowling alley with semiautomatic pinsetters. This required a pin boy to collect the pins and drop them into a pin-setting machine, sometimes narrowly avoiding a scattered pin or ball. Later the owners opened Liberty Lanes in Rondout. A Dodge dealership took over the building pictured, which was demolished in 2009. A new commercial development stands in its place.

The first Masonic lodge in Libertyville was organized in 1867 with about 20 members. The Masonic Temple in Libertyville was built in 1931–1932 at a cost of around $50,000. John Scribbings of Glencoe was the architect, and Ben Miller, as president of the Masonic Temple Association, supervised the project. In the 1950s, the Mormon Church met here. Also the youth groups, crinoline-wearing Rainbow Girls, and tuxedoed DeMolays held events at the space. It continues to be used for fraternal organization meetings.

Early village fathers recognized the importance of rail service to village growth. They convinced the Chicago, Milwaukee, and St. Paul Railroad to extend the end of the line from Rondout to Libertyville in 1880. This railroad underpass was constructed in 1899–1900 when the Chicago, Milwaukee, and St. Paul Railroad extended its passenger line to Fox Lake and Wisconsin on the Janesville-Madison division. The track parallels Newberry Avenue, and the rail bridge spans Second Street at Oak Spring Road.

Libertyville's development soared when a spur of the Chicago, Milwaukee, and St. Paul Railroad brought the first train to town in 1880. As rail activity continued to expand in the 1900s, the original depot on First Street was dedicated to freight. This passenger depot was constructed at the northeast corner of Milwaukee and Newberry Avenues. The passenger depot was demolished in 1978 when Metra built a new station on the west side of Milwaukee. Marathon Gas resides here now.

The first Libertyville Post Office was located in a log cabin in 1837. Thereafter it was housed in different businesses, depending upon who the postmaster was. The government erected this building in 1935 when F. W. Hanlon was postmaster. In 1991, the post office moved to a modern facility on Artaius Parkway. The Libertyville Civic Center moved into the building shortly after and is now owned by the village. The Civic Center hosts community events and private parties.

A fire that devastated downtown Libertyville on August 30, 1895, was the stimulus that formed the first fire department, a volunteer unit with a hand-pumped engine. Later, in 1913, a building was proposed on Cook Street to house a horse-drawn engine and village offices. The expanded three-bay fire station pictured here was completed in 1948. Libertyville's current village hall was constructed from this building in 1994. Most of the outer shell was retained, and the bays were converted into windows.

Ansel B. Cook built this home in 1878. Upon his third wife's death, the property was turned over to the village to be used as a library. After renovations, including a stucco facade and stately columns, Cook Memorial Library opened in 1921. It served as the library until 1968, when a larger facility was built on the property. Since then, it has been home to the Libertyville-Mundelein Historical Society and operates as a Victorian museum.

The village dedicated the gazebo in June 1980. It is a replica of the Adler estate gazebo, originally located on the banks of the Des Plaines River in Adler Park. In 1978, the Libertyville Village Board considered moving and restoring the old Adler gazebo to the Central Park as a gateway to the downtown heritage area. The replica was designed after vandals burned the original gazebo in 1979. It is featured on many town signs as a symbol of Libertyville.

Paul Ray opened the Ray Funeral Home in 1913. By 1937, he moved his business into the Victorian home pictured here. His son-in-law Ken Burnett assisted him in the business, resulting in a name change to Ray-Burnett. During the 1950s, the funeral home offered private ambulance service and modern chapels. After Ray's death in 1963, the business became Burnett Home. Over the years, many renovations greatly expanded the facility. Paul Dane, an apprentice of Burnett's, currently owns the establishment, which is now the Burnett-Dane Funeral Home.

In 1948, Bernice and John McMurrough opened the McMurrough Funeral Chapel in the former Boehm home. In their sixth year, they completed an air-conditioned addition. It included a large chapel with seating for 200, a reception area, a casket display room, and a preparation room. Private ambulance service was also offered in the 1950s. In 1965, a second renovation brought it to its current size. After John's death in 1978, his son Mark (current owner) took over the business.

Designed by architect H. V. von Holst and built on farmland, Condell Memorial Hospital opened in 1928 at the bequest of Elizabeth Condell and with contributions from Samuel Insull and the community at large. Condell survived the Depression and World War II to successfully expand in 1952 (the Noble Wing) and in 1954 (Hough Maternity Wing). The Penwasciz program, unique to Condell, continues to encourage students to enter the medical field. Today Condell is proud to be the area's only Level I trauma center.

Lakeside Cemetery was established in the early 1840s, within a few years of the arrival of the area's first settlers. Presumably it was named for its proximity to Butler Lake. The distinctive wrought-iron entrance is all that remains of a fence that surrounded the cemetery in the 1800s. By the 1950s, the old cemetery had become a lesson in local history with early pioneers, Civil War veterans, and prominent citizens all resting here. It is still in operation.

Historical Business Index

Bringin' Home the Bacon

Be True to Your School

Sunday Go to Meetin'

Takin' Care of Business